bar napkins
for beginners

by graham smith

illustrated by fernando gallegos

SADIE
GIRL
PRESS

ISBN-13: 978-0692432266
ISBN-10: 0692432264
copyright 2015
graham smith
published by
sadie girl press
cover and inside art by
fernando gallegos

table of contents

if it's wednesday, it must be haiku

majestic aether
wheeling stars, planets, and moons
through their perfect rounds

angels playing near
the sun return to flight school
singed but not fallen

black velvet wings at
midnight stir cravings for a
wet kiss on the neck

pushing up through snow
lusciously colorf'lly bold
the first blooms of spring

flickering torchlight
bison running silently
deep inside the cave

costa concordia
"lord jim" re-told off
the tuscan coast, a captain
who needs redemption

torches and pitchforks
at the castle gates, again!
what is it this time?

blade dipped in poison
the wound deep, blood turned to smoke
may be late for work

cutting a path through
the steaming jungle, back to
a primeval world

emeralds lying
in the river bed, guarded
by sly crocodiles

limping from croc bites
with both hands full of treasure
trying to get home

too weak from wounds and
fever to chop through even
one more vine

fresh white bones and dark
green gems glisten quietly
in the cleansing rain

waving goodbye, then
running to the bow, sailing
on to a new life

shimmering faintly
on a moonless night, an ice
island looms ahead

staring quietly
at the hearth's embers, white star
telegram in hand

a gull flutters and
lands on a broken deck chair
floating far from land

a lifetimes 's treasures
piled in plastic bags on a
borrowed shopping cart

moon walking across
the dark stage through pools of light
exiting house right

facing down a tank
unarmed, defining courage
for generations

walked past a storm drain
heard splishy splashy footsteps
echo from below

blank faces lit blue
while texting, not talking with
friends one foot away

i'm thumbing, she stops,
where you going? i say hell
she smiles, says hop in!

pawn to Queen's Knight four
bishop takes pawn, no big deal
except to the pawn

looked around for a
graceful exit, found that it
had always been there

the needle gently
coaxes a straus waltz from the
spinning cylinder

some readings
at the ugly mug

childhood memory
the old door-to-door
scissor sharpener man was
missing four fingers

a journey to the stars
wilshire, beverly
melrose, santa monica
sunset, hollywood

scratched vinyl
skipping back to old
songs, breaking his record for
repeating mistakes

literary figure of speech
he told his friends that
he was hanging in there, which
was how they found him

layer cake grave
at her service, each
of her children buried a
different mother

tantriku master
he's arranged his
syllables into seventeen
new positions

he slipped his jacket
under her to save soft skin
from a carpet burn

when she enters a
room, all of the colors of
life flow around her

tautology
a journey of a
thousand paces begins with
a single mile

a simile is
like a smile, only it is
spelled differently

16

winter
deep silence
a blanket of fresh snow
outside the door

razor waiting
winter tap water,
slowly warming, pours across
his sleepy fingers

open mic at the north pole
santa smoked a bowl
and, eyes twinkling, read a poem from
his naughty list

the past bullied its
way into the present
with brass knuckles

the tragical presidency of william henry harrison
in this haiku play
the curtain rises, and the
prologue is the end

a slightly rusty irony
navajo patterned
rugs, loomed in calcutta: so
columbus was right

19

island twilight
the weathered idol's
last, untended flame is washed
away by the rain

were-owl
every full moon
hedwig leaves a fresh trail of
house-elf bones and blood

as delicate and
graceful as a brush painting
cranes on rice paper

sea changes

canvas snaps full, lines
strain, as trade winds pull the prow
west through foaming waves

he sails a stormy
sea of strangers to a small
island of friendship

the afternoon sun
paves a golden road over
the westerly sea

the sneak thief sun
drops down below the clouds
steals away the day

where land and sea meet
stone rises in strength, cradles
a beacon of light

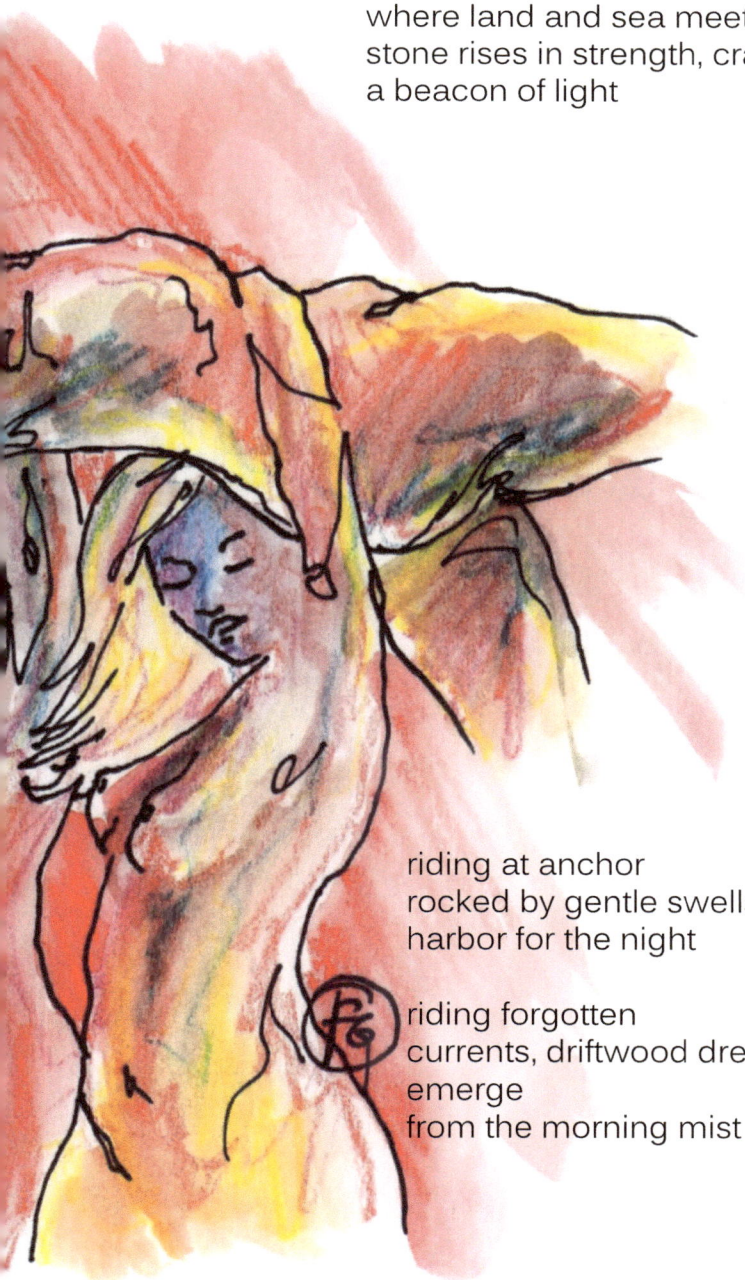

riding at anchor
rocked by gentle swells, a safe
harbor for the night

riding forgotten
currents, driftwood dreams
emerge
from the morning mist

running at high tide -
wet sand and kelp, surf soaked ai
morning's slate washed clean

a school of thoughts, glimpsed
briefly, flash through kelp, vanish
before being caught

currents swirl tresses
waves froth over supple scales
a merman's wet dream

the breakers just seem
to advance as they cover
the retreating tide

pale slate winter sky -
charcoal smudges tinged with pir
scud low in the west

the patient osprey
scans the surf each morning for
her favorite friend

a dark from rises
through the living blue, breaches
near a passing friend

sea and sky
reflect each other in
muted shades of you

she writes from deep in
the pocket - deftly glides
along passion's crest

the wind of passage
tangles her hair, dolphins
play on the bow wave

the warm gulf stream soothes,
lovingly embraces,
fills her lungs

the sea heals the earth's
fresh wounds, and cools her rivers
of incandescence

sailing awakens
memories of the sea
i should not have

i dreamt
too deeply
and drowned

trying to push our
longboat out through the surf, the
sea beyond beckons

cutting swiftly through
the swells, our lee rail awash,
the joy of our wake

our gauze muffled oars
swept us silently towards
the bone white beach

stranded on this isle
hoping to find cannabis
and not cannibals

smashed timbers on the
beach, sea soaked crates, remains
of a shipwrecked life

9

acknowlegements

the section "if it's wednesday, it must be haiku" previously appeared in one-time photo collection assembled by martha duncan.

the section "sea changes" was previoulsy published in the anthology, *a poet is a poet no matter how tall, episode II, attack of the poems.*

some of the poems in this book were previously published individually in the following:

slam in the ribs poetry night
2014 san gabriel valley poetry calendar
50 haikus
a poet is a poet no matter how tall
cadence collective: year one anthology
gutters & alleyways: perspectives on poverty and struggle

with deep appreciation to sarah thursday for herding these haiku cats onto the pages of a book. also thanks to fernando gallegos, who draws his art from many wells. thank you to nadia, for basho; rudy, for website fun; tara, for objectivity; martha, for the book; jim for thematic suggestions; amber for manuscript suggestions; ben & steve, for poetry idiocy, and all the other hosts of readings, salons and workshops where poetry can be heard, including jim & larry, jaimes, murray & sarah, ed & joanne, daniel & lori, raundi, danielle, denise, christian & steve, zack & karie, nancy & alex, eric, peggy, thea and to the poets, for sharing their voices and the audiences, for listening

about the author

graham smith is an ancient rhymer whose history is shrouded in the mists of time. he may have moved to long beach under the cover of a marine layer. allegedly a former lawyer, he has an affinity for brief poetry. he and his stout companions have been known to frequent coastal taverns, where he sometimes writes three line poems on bar napkins.

about the artist

fernando gallegos is a long beach artist born and raised. he is heavily inspired by the human form and always searching to evoke the feeling of movement and emotion. "i love the power of the brain, to take a simple stroke of color on paper and piece it together to an image with depth and feeling" find more info and keep updated at:

facebook\fernando.gallegos.lbc   instagram\@fgraphix

www.ingramcontent.com/pod-product-compliance
Lightning Source LLC
Chambersburg PA
CBHW041811040426
42449CB00004B/151